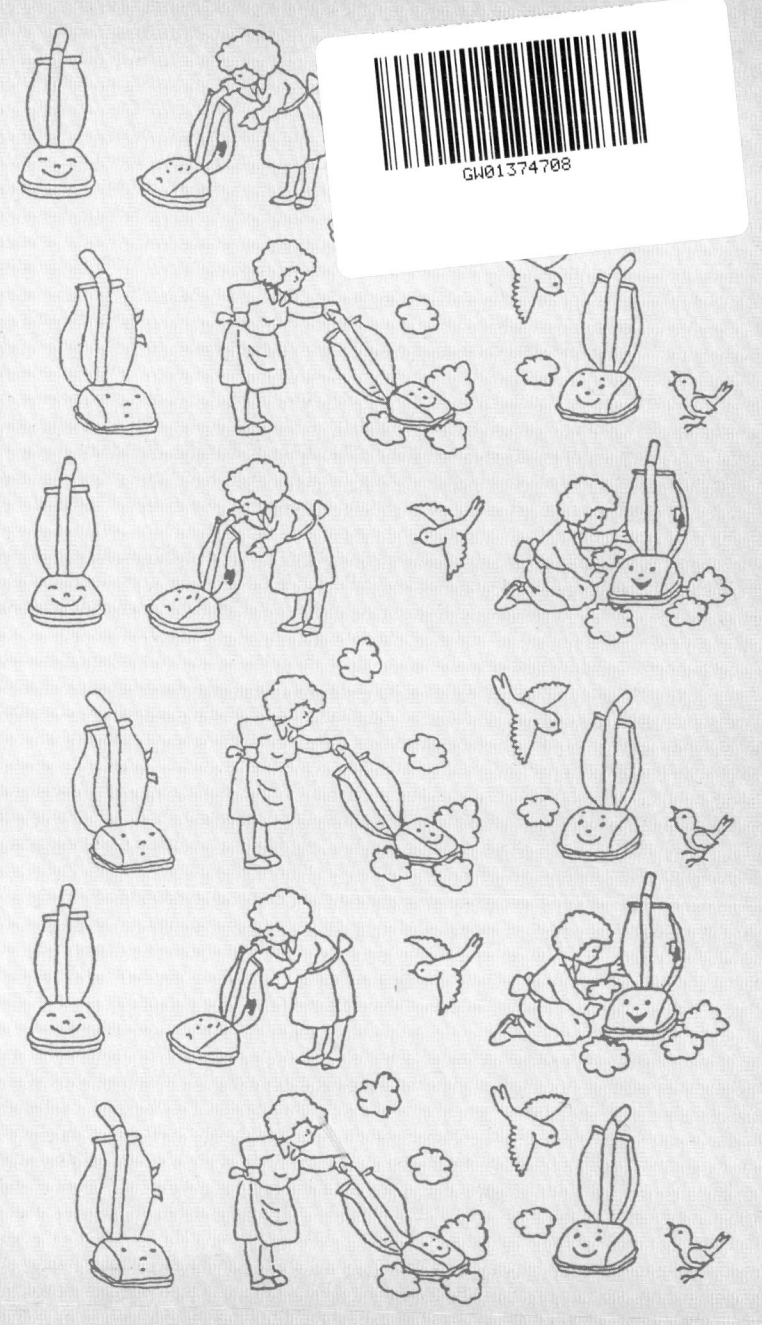

Tommy is Mrs Merryweather's vacuum cleaner, and he becomes a special friend to the blackbirds that live in the garden...

Tommy
and the Blackbirds

A Bedtime Story

by Constance C Jones
illustrated by Gill Guile

Copyright © 1989 by World International Publishing Limited.
All rights reserved.
Published in Great Britain by World International Publishing Limited,
An Egmont Company, Egmont House, P.O.Box 111,
Great Ducie Street, Manchester M60 3BL.
Printed in DDR. ISBN 0 7235 1267 1

A CIP catalogue record for this book is available from the British Library

"Oh dear, oh dear!" said Mrs Merryweather, as her old vacuum cleaner started blowing dust all over the house instead of sucking it up.

Mrs Merryweather called her cleaner Tommy, and it was the silliest cleaner you could ever hope to meet.

Tommy was a very old cleaner and he had been cleaning up Mrs Merryweather's house for as long as either of them could remember.

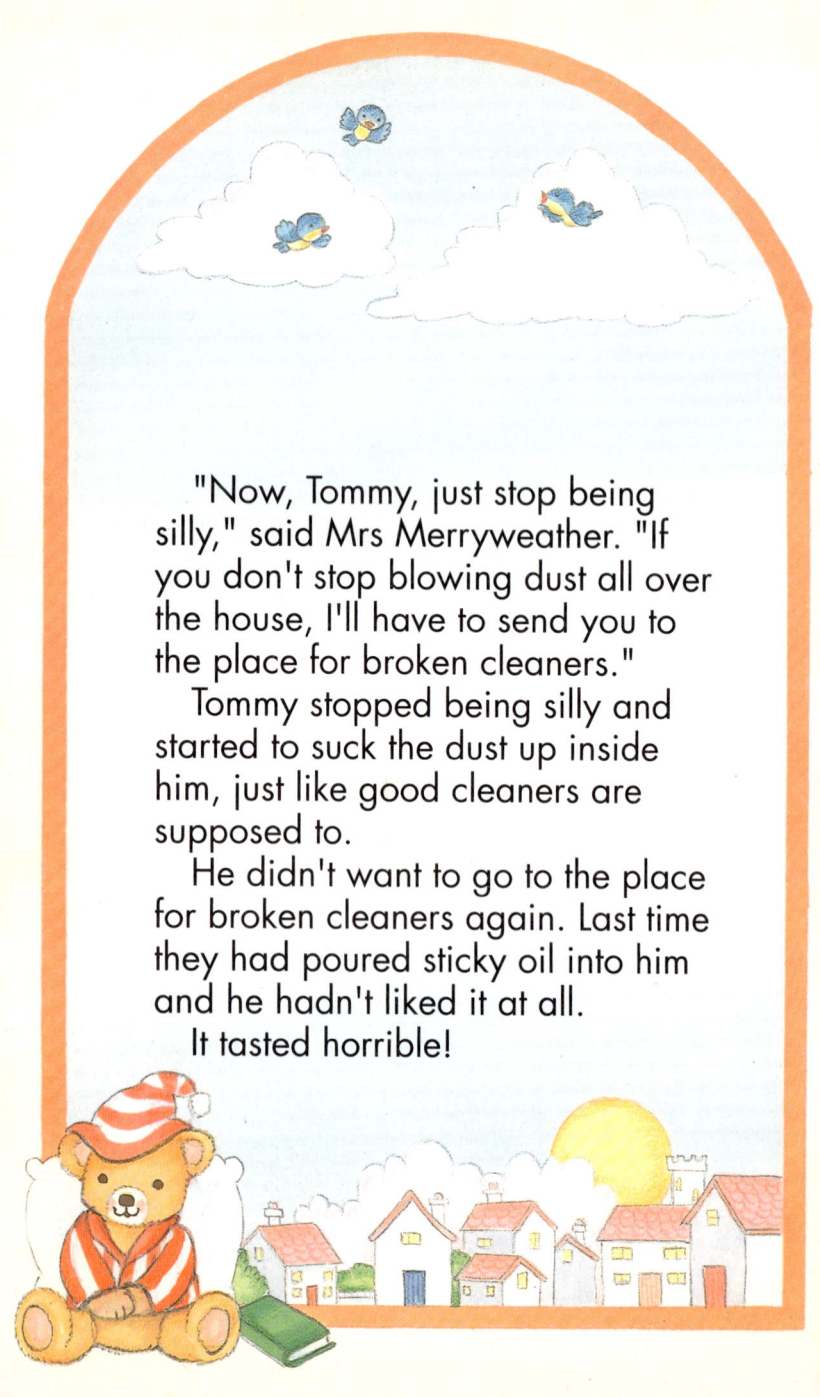

"Now, Tommy, just stop being silly," said Mrs Merryweather. "If you don't stop blowing dust all over the house, I'll have to send you to the place for broken cleaners."

Tommy stopped being silly and started to suck the dust up inside him, just like good cleaners are supposed to.

He didn't want to go to the place for broken cleaners again. Last time they had poured sticky oil into him and he hadn't liked it at all.

It tasted horrible!

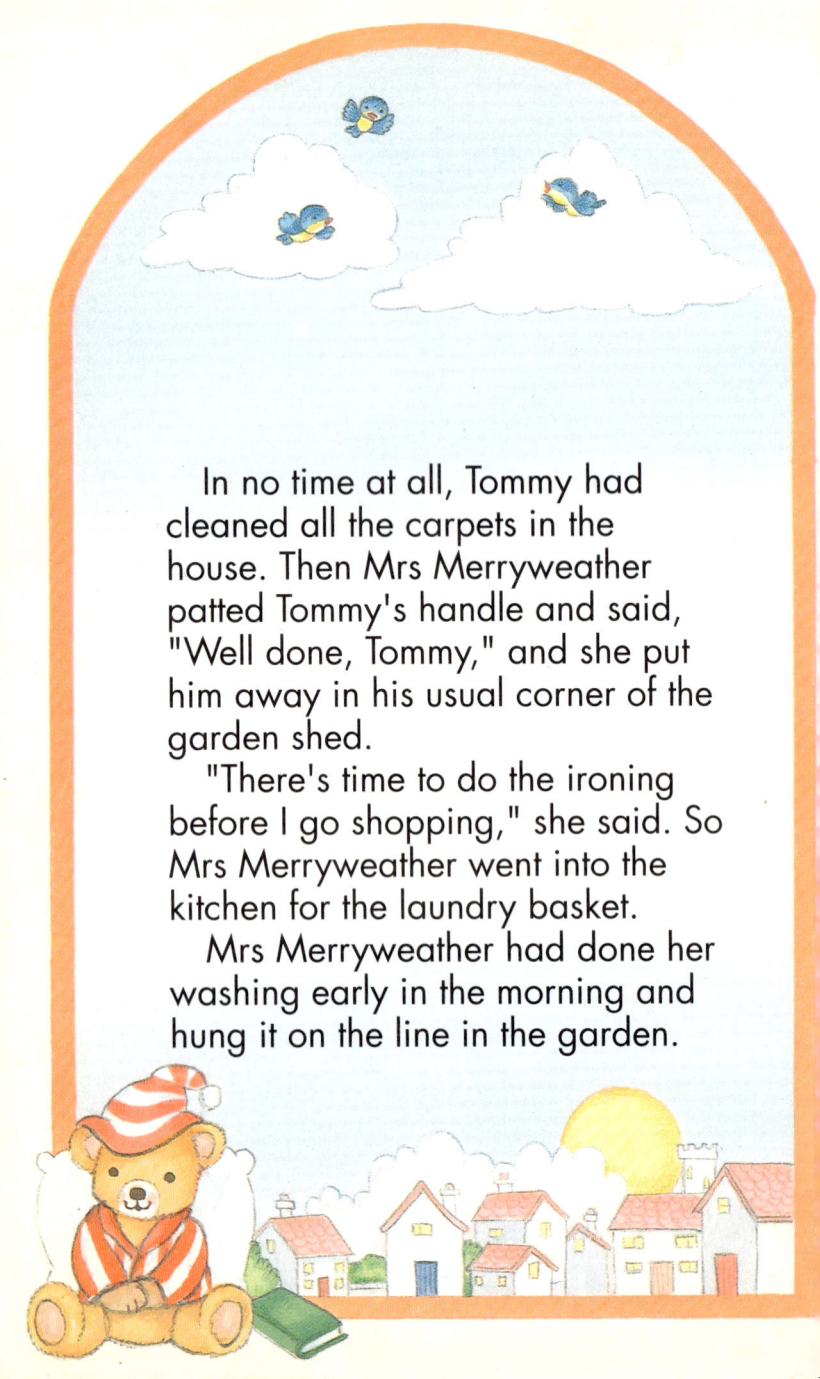

In no time at all, Tommy had cleaned all the carpets in the house. Then Mrs Merryweather patted Tommy's handle and said, "Well done, Tommy," and she put him away in his usual corner of the garden shed.

"There's time to do the ironing before I go shopping," she said. So Mrs Merryweather went into the kitchen for the laundry basket.

Mrs Merryweather had done her washing early in the morning and hung it on the line in the garden.

But, oh! What a shock Mrs Merryweather had when she went out to the clothes line. All her washing had been pulled off the line and thrown on the grass!

She knew who had done it.

"Oh, Blackie Blackbird, you are the naughtiest bird I have ever known," she said as she began to pick her clothes up.

Sitting in a tree in the garden, Blackie Blackbird looked down at the mischief he had done.

He chirped and chirped.

Poor Mrs Merryweather. Between Tommy and Blackie she really was having problems today.

She had often thought of buying a new cleaner. But what would happen to Tommy? She couldn't bear it if the dustbin-men put him on their lorry. And really, he hadn't been *too* silly lately.

Mrs Merryweather had often seen Blackie Blackbird perched on Tommy's handle in the garden shed. How nice it was for them to be such good friends.

But as the days went by, Tommy became sillier and sillier. And each time Mrs Merryweather went to fetch him from the garden shed, Blackie Blackbird started to chirp loudly and fly all around Tommy as he went into the house.

As well as blowing dust all over Mrs Merryweather's carpets, he started making terrible noises.

Mrs Merryweather had to shout to make herself heard!

Then, to her horror, she noticed a small hole in Tommy's side.

"Oh, Tommy. How can I keep my carpets clean with you looking like this?" said Mrs Merryweather in a loud voice.

Tommy's heart sank. What was Mrs Merryweather going to do with him? Surely she wouldn't let the dustbin-men take him away?

Mrs Merryweather put Tommy back in the shed.

When Blackie Blackbird came to see Tommy, he said, "Cheer up, I have found myself a wife and she wants to meet you."

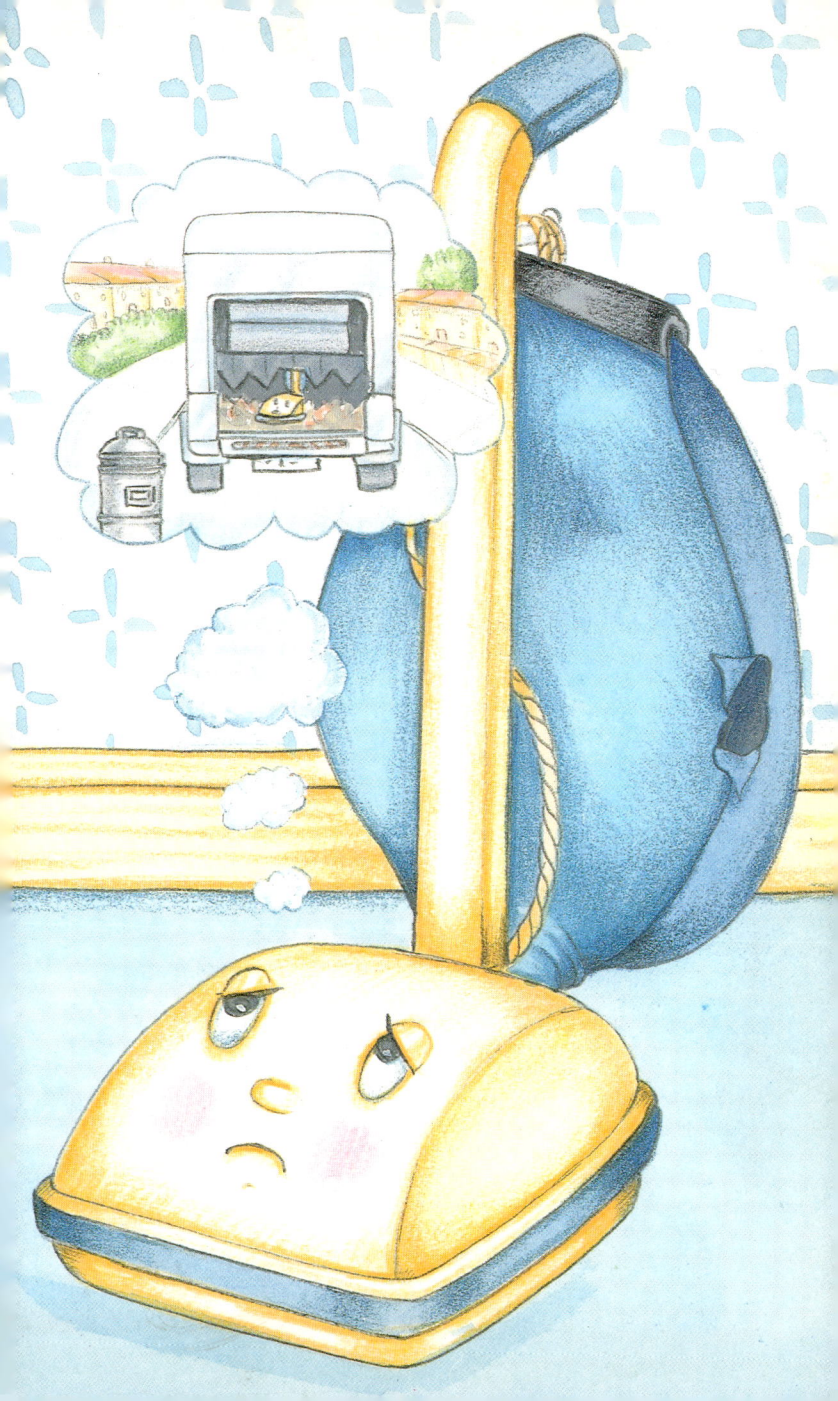

Later that day, Blackie Blackbird and his wife flew into the shed and landed on Tommy's handle.

"This is Mrs Blackie," said Blackie Blackbird.

"I am so sorry you are upset," she sang sweetly to Tommy. "I think we can make you feel better."

The two blackbirds flew around inside the garden shed, chirping and singing to each other. This did make Tommy feel better, and as he smiled, the little hole in his side grew a bit bigger.

Next day, Mrs Merryweather's sister telephoned her with some exciting news.

"I've just bought a new cleaner," said Mrs Merryweather's sister, "and I was wondering if you would like my old one. It still works quite well, and will be better than that old cleaner you have."

"Oh, yes please!" said Mrs Merryweather to her sister. "Tommy has gone so silly that he doesn't clean at all now. He just blows dust all over the carpets!"

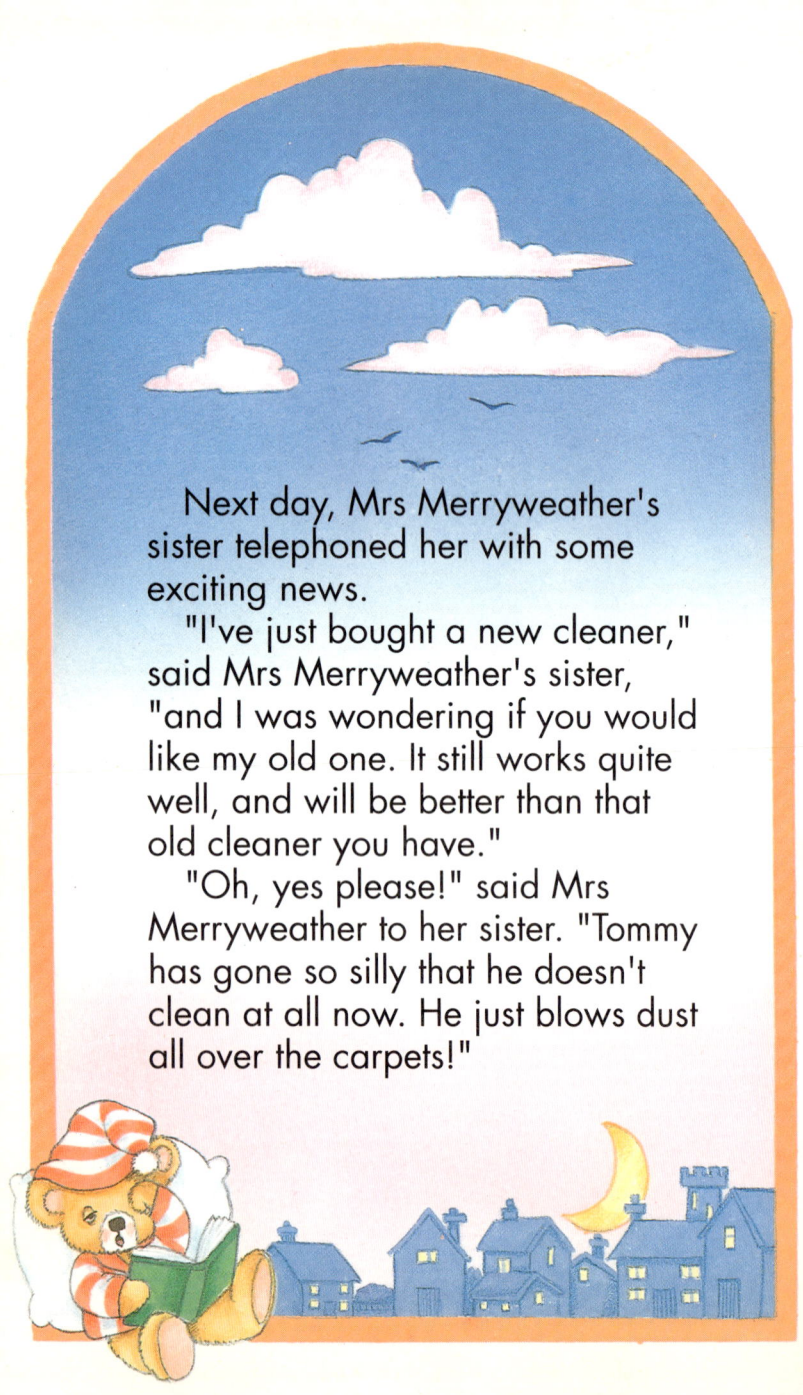

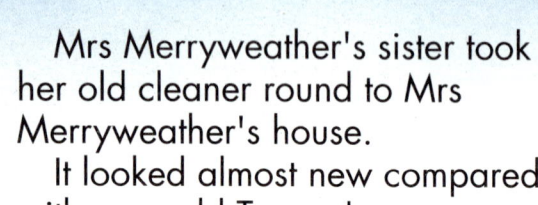

Mrs Merryweather's sister took her old cleaner round to Mrs Merryweather's house.

It looked almost new compared with poor old Tommy!

Mrs Merryweather decided not to give Tommy to the dustbin-men after all.

She left him in the shed, and kept her new cleaner inside the house, so that Tommy would not be upset.

The new cleaner kept Mrs Merryweather's carpets nice and clean.

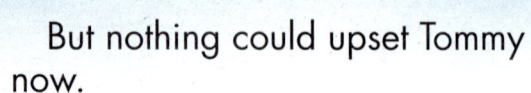

But nothing could upset Tommy now.

Something wonderful had happened to him while he had been left all alone.

One morning, Mrs Merryweather was in the garden shed when she heard much chirping coming from *inside* Tommy.

Mrs Merryweather looked at Tommy. Sitting on his handle were Blackie Blackbird and Mrs Blackie.

"Whatever do we have here, Tommy?" said Mrs Merryweather.

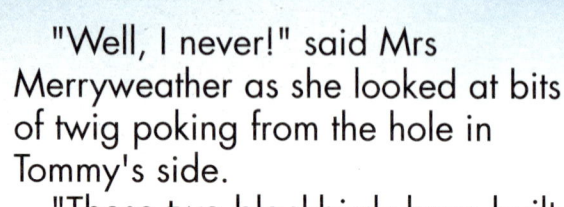

"Well, I never!" said Mrs Merryweather as she looked at bits of twig poking from the hole in Tommy's side.

"Those two blackbirds have built a nest inside you. And there are five baby blackbirds in the nest!" she said.

"You will never have to clean carpets again, Tommy," said Mrs Merryweather. "You can stay here as a nesting place instead."

Tommy smiled. Everything had turned out well after all.